almost 12

almost 12

The Story of Sex

**Tyndale House
Publishers, Inc.**

WHEATON, ILLINOIS

Kenneth N. Taylor

Copyright © 1968, 1995 by Tyndale House Publishers
All rights reserved

First edition, 1968
Second edition, 1991
Third edition, 1995

More than 400,000 copies in print through 35 printings

Cover photo copyright © 1995 by Jim and Mary Whitmer.
Interior illustrations copyright © 1995 by Chris Duke.
Interior photo credits: Brad Baskin 53; Cleo Photography 48-49; Barbara Comnes 3;
Jean-Claude LeJeune 16-17, 62; Marilyn Nolt 28-29; Tara C. Patty 18-19; Skjold
Photographers 6-7; Jim Steere 58-59; Shawn Weimer 22-23, 24-25, 46, 54-55, 60;
Jim Whitmer 2, 4-5, 50, 56-57; Terry Wild 15, 36-37, 45; Neena M. Wilmot 30-31.

Scripture verses are taken from *The Living Bible*, copyright © 1971 owned by
assignment by KNT Charitable Trust. All rights reserved.

ISBN 0-8423-1071-1

Printed in the United States of America

01 00 99 98 97 96
7   6   5   4   3   2

Note to Parents

Many parents are embarrassed about discussing sex with their children, but the children probably aren't nearly so self-conscious about the subject as their parents might expect. They have learned a lot about it in school and via TV, the movies, and many other media. One interesting way to use this book is for your child or children to read it and then explain it back to you page by page. Ask them questions about what they have read, and add your comments that will further clarify anything they have misunderstood or are confused about. Another good way to use the book is to read it together and discuss it as you (or your child) read it aloud. My prayer is that many children will be helped to understand their personal responsibility to God as a result of reading this book.

Ken Taylor

It's fun to be 10 or 11 or 12 years old!

You are almost ready
for middle school or junior high, or perhaps
you are already there. You are learning a lot
at school, and you have friends, birthday
parties, vacations, and school trips.

You are growing taller, too, and you are
learning math, science, health, and history.

You are also learning many ways to be a helpful member of your family—for instance, not complaining when it's your turn to clear the table and do the dishes! And you know about staying healthy by eating the right foods, getting enough sleep, and wearing a bicycle helmet.

Your opportunities for service in the church and youth group are no doubt growing, too. When the Lord Jesus was twelve years old, it was said of Him that He grew in favor with His friends and neighbors and with God. This means He was becoming more and more helpful and well-loved by all who knew Him. I hope this is your experience, too.

The purpose of this book is to talk about sex—a subject that is becoming more and more interesting and important to you. You see this subject all the time on TV and hear about it in the "Top 10" hits of the week. It seems as if the whole world is talking and singing about sex. Some people even like to look at pictures of naked and almost naked women and men in magazines. Sex is discussed in health class, and some kids talk about it at school and even

tell dirty jokes to make their friends laugh. And you are hearing a lot of talk about AIDS, "safe sex," condoms, and homosexuals (or "gays").

Almost 12 is a book for Christian kids and others who want to know what God says about sex, so they can do what is right and can please Him.

Growing up may remind you that

once you were a tiny baby.

Most fathers and mothers want their boys and girls, when they are about your age, to review with them the amazing way God makes babies. You know a lot about this already, but it's a good idea to talk over what you know and perhaps learn even more.

Before you were a baby, where were you?

How did you get here?

I think you know the answer: You started as an egg inside your mother's body, an egg no bigger than the dot on this *i!* You grew quietly and slowly for nine months, in the part of your mother's body called the uterus. You were protected there from bumps and jolts. All those months your mother and father thought a lot about the day you would be born. They prepared a special place for you in their house, and they got the furniture and clothing you would need after you were born. Then at last, that great day came— your birthday!

Here is a diagram showing how a mother's appearance changes as her baby grows bigger and bigger inside her body.

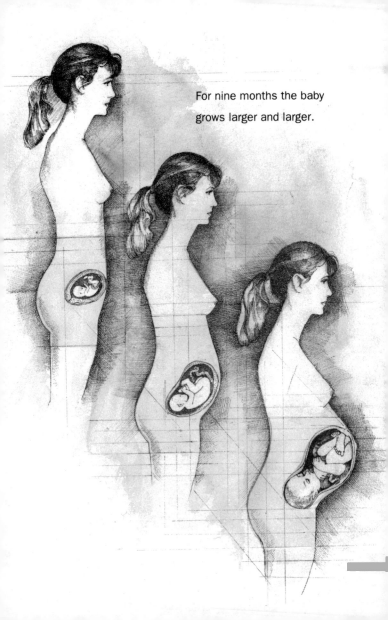

For nine months the baby
grows larger and larger.

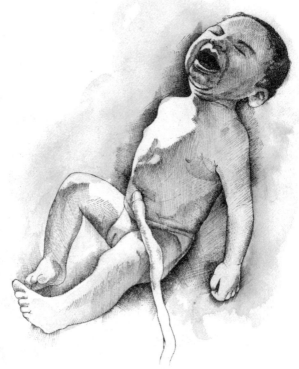

The umbilical cord
connects the baby to its mother.

While a baby is growing inside the mother, it does not eat through its mouth or breathe through its nose. Instead, a special blood vessel (the umbilical cord) is attached to both the mother and baby to provide the baby with nourishment and oxygen from the mother's blood supply. Your navel (or "belly button") is where your own umbilical cord was attached, connecting you to your mother while you were inside her body. Her blood provided oxygen and nutrition for your body so that you could live and grow.

One of the things that happens right after a baby is born is that the doctor cuts that cord, because from then on the baby can breathe and eat independently. Sometimes the doctor lets the baby's father cut the cord, which is pretty exciting for him because it lets him take an active part in his baby's birth.

I know you don't remember your birthday, so here are some of the details!

On the day you were ready to be born,
your mother's body knew this was the right
time and began to push you out where she
could at last hold you in her arms! Strong
muscles inside her started forcing you slowly down through the vagina—the passageway God has provided for birth. Even though
you were very small, you were much larger
than the passageway. The vagina (also
called the birth canal) gradually expanded
during the time your body was moving from
the uterus. All of this pushing and expand-
ing caused pains for your mother, called

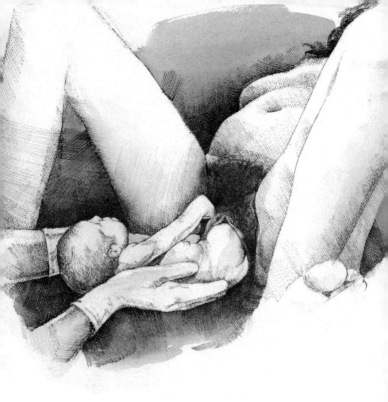

labor pains. Your mother may have been
given some medicine to ease this pain,
although many babies are born without any
medication being used.

Your father's encouragement helped a
lot. He probably reminded your mother how
to breathe in the right way, to relax at some
times, and push hard at other times.

This whole process of giving birth usually takes several hours. But at just the right time, you finally came out of your mother's body. You were born! It was **your birthday!**

The doctor and nurses and your parents were all waiting to meet you. Everyone waited eagerly for your first cry because that showed that you were breathing. Then your mother and father got to hold you for the first time. What a glad moment! For your mother, all the months of waiting and even the labor pains were forgotten because of her love for you and her joy that you were born.

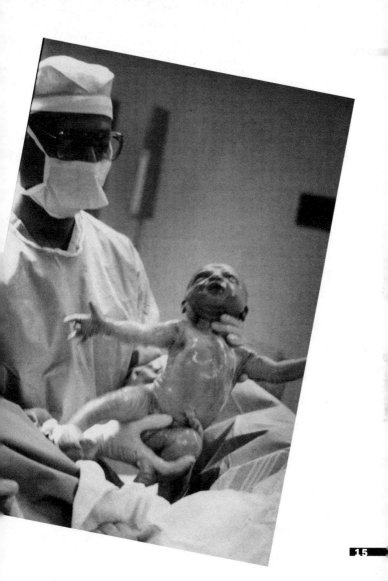

While most babies are born in the way described above, some women are not able to deliver a baby that way. If a doctor thinks it might not be safe for her to have her baby through the vagina, the doctor will decide to do a kind of surgery called a "cesarean section." Perhaps that is the way you were born. If you were, the doctor gave your mother an anesthetic to put her to sleep or to make her drowsy. Then he made an incision in her abdomen and lifted you out through the incision.

Whichever way you were born, your father was so proud of you that he could hardly wait to brag about you to all of the family and friends who had been waiting for you, too. After he telephoned family members with the good news, he probably took some pictures of you right away so he could show them to everyone.

Why do you think he was so happy?

You were too little to play with. All you could do was eat and sleep and cry—and use lots and lots of diapers! But he was proud and happy because you were his!

Your father

was proud and happy because you were his! You never would have become a baby inside your mother if it hadn't been for your father. You started as a tiny egg inside one of your mother's ovaries, but that egg would not have begun to grow if it hadn't been for your father's part in making it become the living, growing baby that you were. We'll talk about your father's part later in this book. Without his help the egg would have died.

But how did you get inside your mother in the first place? These diagrams give the basic information. You began inside your mother as an egg the size of the period at the end of this sentence. God has a marvelous way of changing such a tiny egg into a wonderful newborn baby, nine months later. I'll tell you how it happened.

On the next page is a diagram of a **girl's** sexual organs. If you are a girl, this is what you look like inside:

Fallopian tubes

Beginning when a girl is between ten and fifteen years old, or sometimes even older, an egg leaves an ovary each month and travels through a Fallopian tube into her uterus. If a woman's egg unites with a man's sperm in the Fallopian tube, the egg begins to grow into a baby.

Ovaries

Every woman has two of these inside her body, one at each side of her lower abdomen. She has thousands of eggs in each ovary. They are almost too small to see, much smaller than the head of a pin.

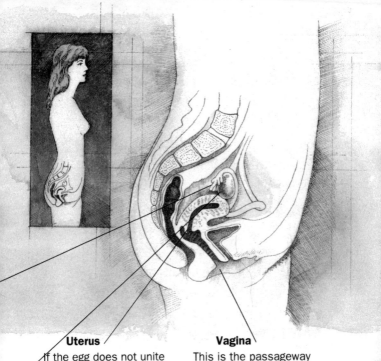

Uterus

If the egg does not unite with a sperm, it leaves the uterus after a few days and goes out of the woman's body, along with some blood, through her vagina. This slow bleeding each month is called menstruation, and it happens about every 28 days. The bleeding continues for four to seven days. These days are called her "menstrual period," or just "her period."

Vagina

This is the passageway into a woman's body at the front, between her legs. The egg and blood leave her body through this passageway. This is also the opening where a baby comes out of the mother's body when it is time to be born. The outside opening of the vagina is just behind the opening through which a woman urinates.

A woman has two ovaries inside her body, one at each side in the lower abdomen. Thousands of eggs almost too small to see are contained in her ovaries. When a girl is from 10 to 15 years old, or older, one of these eggs will move out of one of the ovaries each month and will move through the Fallopian tubes into her uterus.

If a sperm joins with an egg in the Fallopian tube, the egg starts to grow into a baby. This is called conception. But if there is no sperm, the egg goes out through the vagina along with some blood. This slow flow of blood each month is called menstruation. It usually happens about every 28 days and continues for four to seven days.

The reason
the flow from
the uterus con-
tains blood is that
during the 28-day men-
strual cycle, the uterus grows a
cushiony lining containing extra blood cells,
to be a safe and comfortable place for a baby
to grow if conception takes place. If conception doesn't happen—that is, if an egg and a
sperm do not unite to start a baby—that lining leaves the uterus and becomes part of
the menstrual flow. This passage of blood is
not dangerous and doesn't mean that there
is any injury to the woman's body.

The beginning of menstruation is an exciting time for a girl because it shows that her body is getting ready for her to become a grown-up woman. A girl should learn all she can about menstruation before it begins so she can be prepared and not be frightened or worried about it. It is neither a sickness nor a "curse," as some foolishly call it. It is a normal part of growing toward adulthood.

During the days of her period, a woman wears an absorbent pad, called a sanitary napkin, inside her underwear to absorb the blood. Some women prefer to use a tampon instead, which is a roll of absorbent material that is inserted into the vagina to absorb the flow of blood. If menstruation begins while a girl is at school and she is not prepared for it, she should ask a woman teacher or the school nurse for the necessary supplies.

Menstruation is sometimes painful. Some girls experience a backache or abdominal cramping on the first day, which is entirely normal. Your mother or school nurse can advise you about what to do if you have any pain. All the usual health rules about getting enough rest, drinking plenty of water, and doing moderate exercise will help to make your periods a normal —not scary— experience.

Now we'll talk about a **boy's** sex organs. On the opposite page is a diagram of them.

Testicle

There are two of these. They are firm and rubbery and are about the size of marbles. They lie inside a sac called the scrotum. The testicles produce millions of cells called sperm that are too small to see without a microscope. One of these sperm must unite with a woman's egg before the egg can begin to grow into a baby.

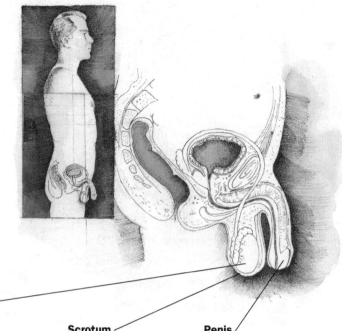

Scrotum

This is a soft sac containing the testicles. This sac is outside the man's body, in front, and hangs down just behind the penis.

Penis

This is where the man's sperm leave his body. This organ is also for urination.

Most of a man's sex organs are outside parts of his body. Between his legs is his penis, which is not only a sex organ but is also the organ through which the bladder empties during urination. Behind the penis is a sac called the scrotum, which contains two balls the size of marbles, called testicles, that produce sperm. Sperm are the living cells that are essential for making a baby. When one of these cells unites with an egg in a woman's body a baby begins.

Sometimes when a boy is only a few days old, a very minor operation may be performed to cut away the skin folds ("foreskin") surrounding the tip of the penis. This is called circumcision and is frequently referred to in the Bible. Some boys are circumcised and others are not. Either way is okay. Being circumcised or not does not affect a boy's sexual development or functions.

When a boy is in junior or senior high school, his body starts to become sexually mature. Although his penis is usually soft and flabby, now it will sometimes become erect and hard for a few minutes, and push out against the front of his pants or pajamas. This is called an erection.

When this happens while he is sleeping, he may have dreams about girls, and a thick fluid called semen (which contains sperm) may leave the testicles, where it is made, and come out through the penis. This is called ejaculation. The fluid dries quickly, leaving a trace of color on the pajamas or bedding. This experience is called by several terms: "nocturnal (nighttime) emission," "seminal emission," or, in less technical words, "wet dream."

A wet dream is a normal part of a boy's growing up, and he should not worry about it or feel embarrassed when it happens. His body soon makes more sperm to replace the amount that was ejaculated.

Each boy and girl has his or her own rate of development, and there is no certain age for the changes that occur as a child's body grows into maturity. However, these changes usually begin around age 12 or 13 for girls and a little later for boys.

One of the first changes for a **boy** is the growth of hair around the base of his penis, on his chest, on his upper lip, and under his arms. His voice begins to change to a deeper tone, and his muscles become stronger and better developed.

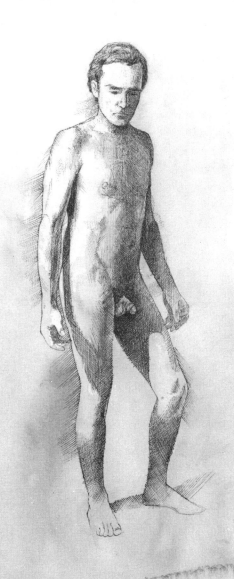

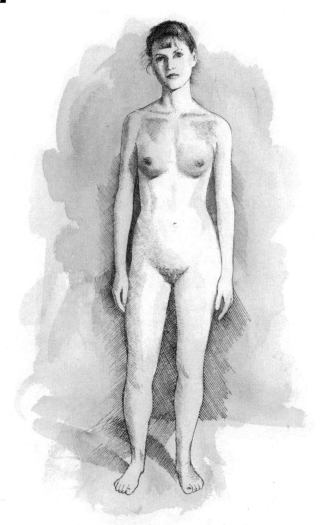

Usually the first sign of change in a **girl**'s body is that her breasts begin to grow a little bit, and she will probably find a small amount of hair growing under her arms and in the genital area (the area between her legs). Then she will begin to have menstrual periods. The menstrual cycle may be very regular right from the start, although it can be somewhat irregular in the first few months.

All of these growing-up signs indicate that boys' and girls' bodies are getting ready for adult responsibilities.

Let's summarize the sexual differences between women and men:

Women's sexual organs are internal. Women produce eggs in their ovaries. Each egg is the size of a tiny grain of sand.

Men's sexual organs are mostly external. Their testicles produce microscopic sperm, surrounded by a fluid called semen, which is ejaculated through the penis.

A woman's egg cannot become a baby unless it is united with a sperm from the father. This is called fertilization. In other

words, an egg is not fertile unless a sperm
unites with it. This makes us appreciate
how important fathers are. When a baby is
born, he or she is part of the father and part
of the mother and belongs equally to both of
them. Chromosomes in the egg and the
sperm determine the color of the baby's
hair, eyes, and **skin,** the shape of
the **nose** and **ears,** and whether the
baby will be a **boy** or **girl.**

Let's look through a microscope at an **egg**

This drawing of an egg is greatly
enlarged, since an egg is about the
size of a very small grain of sand.

and a **sperm.**

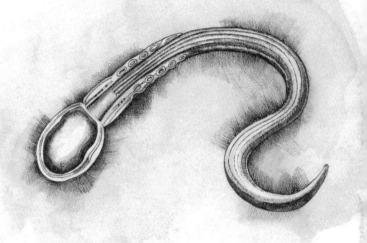

A sperm is much too small to see,
but seen through a microscope it
looks like this illustration.

Here is a diagram to show what happens after the sperm and the egg meet inside the mother's body so that the egg can become a baby. (Remember, the sperm is too small to see, so this is a very big diagram of the very small egg and even smaller wriggling sperm cell that can be seen only

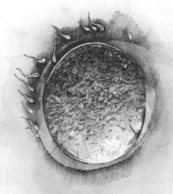

One sperm will break through and unite with the egg.

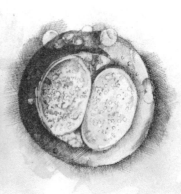

The original egg (joined by a sperm) dividing in half.

through a microscope.)

The second diagram shows the fertilized egg dividing in half.

Then each half divides again and keeps on dividing again and again. Soon the constantly dividing cells become millions of cells, and in a few weeks they take on the recognizable shape of a baby. About four weeks after the egg first begins dividing, the baby's tiny heart begins to beat, and at nine weeks the tiny fingers and toes are formed. The baby is now about one inch long.

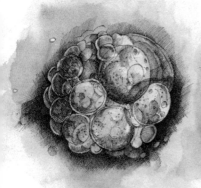

Each half divides again.

As the cells divide, a baby begins to grow.

A baby does not grow by one cell getting bigger and changing its shape, but by each cell dividing into more cells until there are billions of them. In the last diagram, the cells are beginning to look like a baby.

By the third month of growth a baby is three or four inches long. By the fifth month the baby is about a foot long and weighs about one pound. By now the mother may feel the tiny legs kicking!

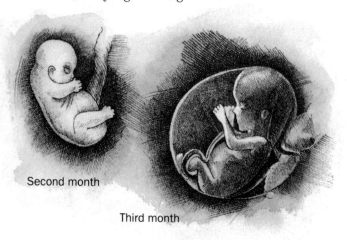

Second month

Third month

By the seventh month, the baby weighs from two to two-and-a-half pounds and moves around a lot inside the uterus.

By the end of the ninth month, when the baby is ready to be born, he or she weighs six to ten pounds and is seventeen to twenty-two

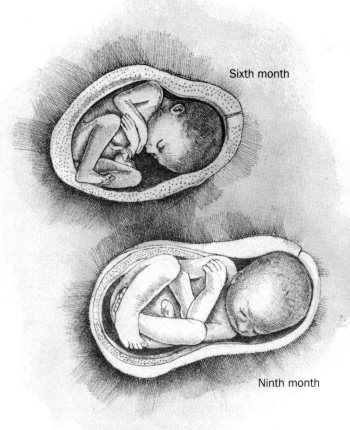

Sixth month

Ninth month

inches long. Originally this tiny egg was much
smaller than the head of a pin! In nine months
it has grown into a strong, squirming, lovable
baby, there inside the mother.

When the baby is ready to be born, the mother's abdominal muscles push it through the vagina and out into the waiting hands of a doctor, nurse, friend, or the baby's father.

How wonderful God is! He makes a baby from an egg the size of a tiny grain of sand and a sperm too tiny to be seen.

Sometimes other kids, and even adults who don't know better, giggle and whisper cheap jokes and silly stories about this wonderful process of being born. Perhaps they are embarrassed because they don't fully understand what sex really means, so they cover up their ignorance by trying to make the facts about sex sound dirty.

The beginning of life is one of the most important and fascinating events in this world. We need to realize what it means for God to create a new life and send it into the world to serve Him. God's marvelous plan for creating new life should cause amazement and thankfulness, not embarrassment!

"How does a man's sperm get into a woman's body?" God made a good plan for this, and it's called sexual intercourse. He intends it to be part of the life of a married couple because when a baby is born it needs both a mother and father to love it, protect it, and provide for it.

At times the husband's penis becomes firm and erect, instead of soft and limp as it usually is, and then it can fit into his wife's vagina. When it is placed there, the husband's seminal fluid, which contains the sperm, flows into her vagina, enabling the sperm to make their way up through the uterus and into the Fallopian tubes to unite with an egg. How wise God was when He made men's and women's bodies so that they fit together during sexual intercourse. You may also be wondering if the sperm from the father become mixed with the urine that also passes through the man's penis. But God made a "shut-off valve" so that when the sperm are passing through the penis, no urine can pass with them.

When a husband and wife unite in this way, they are expressing their love for each other. Sexual intercourse, sometimes called "having sex," gives deep pleasure to both the husband and the wife. They may have sex several times a month, but usually the sperm doesn't find an egg to unite with. That means that conception doesn't take place every time a couple has intercourse. Remember the menstrual cycle? Only at certain times during that 28-day cycle is it possible for an egg to be in the right place to be fertilized by a sperm.

But if the sperm meets an egg and unites with it, a baby begins. The fertilized egg continues its journey into the uterus, where it becomes attached to the soft lining of the wall (that's called implantation) and grows for nine months.

Those nine months are called the gestation period. It is a long time, but the egg and sperm are so small when they unite that it takes that long for them to become eyes, ears, nose, mouth, arms, legs, stomach, skin, bones, and everything else! So nine months is really not so long after all, considering all that happens.

Those are the basic facts about the physical part of sex. But that's not all we need to understand about it. The emotional part is important, too, and we'll talk about that next.

The emotional part of sex is just as important as the physical part. As boys and girls grow up, they are attracted to each other and want to be close friends. Puberty takes place a long time before a boy is ready to be a husband and father or a girl is ready to be a wife and mother. Sexual feelings are experienced by boys and girls before they are emotionally mature and ready for marriage or parenthood. Boys begin to have a desire to see and to touch a girl's breasts and other private parts of her body. And girls have a desire to touch and be touched, too.

If they want to obey God, they won't do these things because these actions can easily lead to having sex, which God forbids until marriage. But the urge is very strong, and the boy and girl may find themselves giving in to their sexual desires. This kind of touching and kissing (called "making out," "necking," "petting," etc.) can easily lead to sexual intercourse, as described earlier in the book. And God says that this is absolutely wrong until marriage. The word for this is *fornication,* and God forbids it.

Assuming that **you want to obey God** and not yield to your strong sexual desires, what should you do to prevent disobeying Him by having sex? Here are some suggestions and rules:

1. The first step is to **know in advance that you are going to have these powerful sexual feelings.** Make the decision ahead of time that you are going to obey what God tells you in the Bible about keeping your life pure. Remember God's rule: Sexual intercourse before marriage is wrong.

2. The second step is to **say *No!*** to anyone who wants to do this with you. Once a boy and girl begin touching each other's

bodies in a sexual way, it is harder and harder to want to stop. So the best thing is not to start in the first place.

One thing that will help a boy and girl not to start being tempted into sexual behavior is to avoid being alone with each other. "Hanging out" with several friends can be fun and harmless, but too much casual "hanging out" in couples, especially alone in a house or a car, is unwise. Staying with groups of friends, being active in church gatherings, having some adults around at parties (especially in private homes)—all these will make it easier to obey God's wise rules about sexual activity.

3. Another very important way to stay pure is to **keep your mind clean.** Guard against reading books and magazines that are sexually exciting, seeing movies or videos with sex scenes, and listening to singers whose songs encourage you to disobey God in these matters.

4. Many young Christians find it helpful to **use a system called "accountability."** This means having a special friend whom you greatly respect for

his or her spiritual maturity and good reputation, and to whom you can talk honestly about your desire to please and obey God. This person might be a parent or the parent of one of your friends, a Christian teacher, an older brother or sister, or the pastor or youth director at your church. It's a good idea to choose a person who is the same sex you are, especially if you want to discuss sexual matters. Ask that person to let you be accountable to him or her, talking over how you are handling the various problems of growing up and praying with you about your needs.

5. Quite apart from the importance of not breaking God's law against sex before marriage, there is the frightening and tragic **possibility that a girl may become pregnant** and will bring a baby into the world long before she and the boy are ready to become parents. This can easily ruin the lives of both the girl and the boy who find themselves in this sad predicament. This problem can present the girl with the temptation to have an abortion— letting a doctor surgically end the pregnancy by killing the unborn baby. Both fornication and murder are sins, so an abortion is never the right solution to a pregnancy.

If a friend of yours disobeys God's law and becomes pregnant, urge her and the

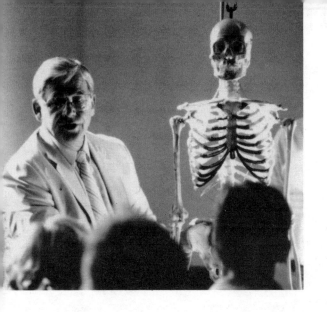

baby's father to consider letting a Christian married couple adopt the baby.

6. A further problem with sexual sin, one that could end your life, is the **ever-present possibility that you will get AIDS,** a disease that has no cure and always leads to death, **or you may get other sexually transmitted diseases** that can do permanent harm to your body. None of this will happen to you if you follow God's laws of *Don't* and *Hands Off.*

Someday God will give you the gift of love for a man or woman who will become your husband or wife.

That seems a long way off, but you will grow up very quickly, and you and your husband or wife will always be glad that you kept your bodies free of sexual diseases and impure behavior. Good marriages are built on respect and friendship just as much as on sexual activity, so you will want to be a person who can be respected and trusted as a friend as well as a sexual partner to your husband or wife.

God has made us to enjoy sex, and it is right and good after marriage. It is pleasant and fun to caress and kiss a person of the opposite sex, but God has made us so that caressing and kissing prepare our bodies to desire to go all the way and have sexual intercourse. Since He has made intercourse to be a part of marriage, it's important to be careful and honorable about the way we behave toward each other before we are married. Doctors and psychologists tell us that when unmarried people have sexual intercourse, it changes their attitude toward each other so much that even if they do marry later on, they may not be able to have a truly trusting relationship. Their guilt may even make them come to despise each other and become enemies and destroy their marriage.

God has made us for Himself. We are His; He bought us when Jesus died on the cross. If you have given yourself to Him and asked Him to be your Savior, you want to honor Him in all that you think and say and do. If you wait until you are married for sexual pleasures, God will reward you for your patience and self-control. In the Bible, in the book of Galatians (chapter 5, verse 23) we learn that if we are Christians, the Holy Spirit lives in us, and He gives us the ability to have self-control.

Give God your body as well as your mind and heart, and keep them pure for Him.

What is peer pressure?

Your "peers" are the people of your own age and social group. *Peer pressure* means wanting to do whatever others in your group or in your school are doing so that you won't be different. You may think you should wear the same kind of clothes the most popular kids wear or you should think and act as they do, even if it is wrong. You may not want to be different, for fear you will be thought weird. The Bible, however, tells us to be very different from those who do wrong. We are to remember that we are children of God, who do what He says instead of doing what "everyone else" says is right. Stand strongly against peer pressure when it is wrong. Stand up for what is right.

What is a virgin?

A virgin is a boy, girl, man, or woman who has never had sexual intercourse. God commands that you remain a virgin until marriage.

What is the difference between fornication and adultery?

Both words mean having sexual intercourse outside of marriage. Adultery is sex with someone who is married to someone else. Fornication is sex between a man and woman or boy and girl who are not married to each other. God says these are serious sins.

What is sexual intercourse?

This is placing a man's penis into a woman's vagina. Other terms for this are "having sex" or "making love." Slang terms you may hear are "doing it" or "going all the way." You may also hear vulgar four-letter words used to describe this act—words we usually call obscene; those words have no place in our vocabulary because they cheapen something God planned to be a beautiful part of married life. Usually these slang and obscene words are used by people who have the idea that sex is something dirty, so they are embarrassed to use the correct terms. Sexual intercourse is not dirty; it is right and good between married partners, but it is otherwise strictly forbidden by God's laws. We will be judged for breaking His law. Even though we know God can forgive us if we are truly sorry for our sins, it is surely best not to sin in the first place.

What is a condom?

A condom is a tube made of latex and shaped like the finger of a glove. It is used to slip over the penis to prevent a man's sperm from passing into a woman's vagina during sexual intercourse. A condom can be used for birth control, to prevent a woman from becoming pregnant.

What does "safe sex" mean?

"Safe sex" refers to the use of a condom during intercourse for protection against getting a sexually transmitted disease, such as AIDS. This is wrongly called "safe sex." It isn't really safe. Many sexually transmitted diseases are spread despite the use of condoms. The only way to be sure of avoiding a sexually transmitted disease is to have intercourse only with one's husband or wife, assuming that neither partner has had intercourse with any other person. How wise God was to protect us with His rules against sexual sins!

What is an abortion?

It is a kind of operation that causes the death of a baby who is still growing inside its mother. A woman may decide to have an abortion because she is not married and doesn't want to take responsibility for the baby she has conceived, or she may be married but just not want to have a child. Either way, she is having her baby killed. It is the law in most states that the unborn baby may be killed at any time during the mother's pregnancy. But even though abortion is legal, it is still murder, and it breaks God's law against murder. Isn't it strange that the law allows a baby to be killed just before its birth, but after it is born, killing it would be illegal!

If an unmarried girl or woman becomes pregnant and cannot take care of her baby properly, she should allow the baby to mature and be born, then arrange for the baby to be adopted by a loving Christian family that can give the child all the care it needs while growing up.

If abortion isn't against the law, how can it be called murder?

The reason abortion can be legal is that the people on the Supreme Court, who decide such things, have ruled that while a baby is still inside the mother's body, it is not really a person; therefore, ending its life is not murder. But an unborn baby is indeed a person, into whose body God has placed an eternal, living soul. Many verses in the Bible talk about how God planned everything about us long before we were born and how He knew us personally while we were still in our mother's body. This is how we know God would not want anyone to kill an unborn baby.

The Bible tells us that God says, "I knew you before you were formed within your mother's womb" (Jeremiah 1:5). Because we believe what the Bible says about life before birth, we know abortion is really murder, breaking one of God's important laws. That's why it is wrong.

My girlfriend says that whatever she does to her body is her own business and she should have the right to have an abortion if she wants to. I think she is wrong, but I don't know how to answer her.

Yes, she is very wrong. Look in your Bible at 1 Corinthians 6:19-20. There we learn that our bodies are not our own but are a place where God's Holy Spirit lives if we are His children. It says, "Your own body does not belong to you. For God has bought you with a great price. So use every part of your body to give glory back to God because he owns it."

Furthermore, an unborn baby is not part of its mother's body (like her appendix or tonsils) but is a separate person with a life (and rights) of its own. Killing that baby is an act of destroying a human life without any regard for the baby's rights.

What does it mean to be "gay"?

Gay is a slang word meaning "homosexual." A woman who is a homosexual is called a lesbian. Men and women who are "gay" get sexual enjoyment from persons of the same sex as themselves. In several places in the

Bible, God tells us that He strictly forbids the practice of homosexuality: "Homosexuality is absolutely forbidden, for it is an enormous sin" (Leviticus 18:22).

Why does God condemn homosexuality?

God created men and women to have a desire to show love to each other through having sex when they are married. Earlier in this book we learned how wise God was to make the husband's body and the wife's body fit together in sexual intercourse, both for their pleasure and so that they can have children.

Sexual acts between members of the same sex are against God's plan, and they are serious sins.

Some people say being gay is just an "alternative lifestyle." Is that true?

They mean that homosexuality is just as good a way to live as heterosexuality (that's what we call it when people want to make love to those of the opposite sex). They say that no one has a right to say one way is better than the other.

But God has the right to say it, and He

says it repeatedly in the Bible. Don't be
fooled by those who claim the Bible doesn't
mean what it clearly says. The gay lifestyle is
not an option. It is wrong.

Does God hate gays?

No, He loves them as much as He loves
other sinners like you and me. But He hates
their sinning. Jesus died on the cross to pay
for their sins and will forgive them if they con-
fess their sins and turn to God for His help.

What is AIDS?
And what do those letters stand for?

AIDS are initials that stand for Acquired
Immunodeficiency Syndrome. This is a fatal
infection usually caused by having sex with
a person who is infected with AIDS. No one
yet knows how to cure people with AIDS.
Because AIDS weakens or destroys the
immune system in the body, people who are
infected with it will eventually get some
dangerous illness. Because they can't fight
the infection, they keep getting sicker and
sicker, and finally they die.

One important way to keep from getting
AIDS is to have sex only with the one person

to whom you are married and who has never had sex with any person who may have had AIDS.

What's the difference between HIV and AIDS?

HIV stands for Human Immunodeficiency Virus, and it is the virus that causes AIDS by attacking and weakening the immune system of the patient. Most patients get it through sexual intercourse with a person who is HIV positive, but the virus can also be transmitted through the use of a syringe ("needle") that was used by an infected person (usually a drug user) or even through a transfusion of infected blood. An unborn baby can get it if the mother is infected with HIV or AIDS. A person who has any reason to think he or she may have HIV should have a blood test. If that test shows that the virus is in the blood, the person is referred to as "HIV positive" and will likely develop AIDS.

I know a guy who is gay, and he says he was born that way and can't help having homosexual feelings. Why is he a sinner if he can't help being gay?

He may desire a male sexual partner, but "feeling like" committing a sin doesn't make it right to do it. For instance, a person might want to steal something or even be angry enough to kill someone, but if he wants to obey God's rules, he won't do it. People who have a desire for sexual activity with a person of the same sex can, with God's help, resist that temptation and refuse to live that lifestyle just as people who are not gay can say no to fornication and adultery.

I've heard that if a boy is sexually aroused it is harmful to him if he doesn't go ahead and have sex with his girlfriend.

No, this is not true. When a boy has an erection, it is because more blood than usual has collected in the blood vessels of the penis, causing it to become larger and harder. This can and does happen to a boy or man frequently, sometimes several times a day. It is not necessary for him to have an ejaculation in order to have the erection go away; this will happen naturally, usually after a few minutes.

But it's also important that a girl be

smart enough and thoughtful enough not to do things with her boyfriends that she knows can be sexually arousing. What are some of those things? Sitting on a boy's lap, deliberately pressing her body against his, dressing immodestly, constantly touching him—all those physical contacts may seem to invite him to respond sexually. In other words, a girl who is a sexual tease may give a boy mixed signals. She may not really intend that he have sexual intercourse with her, but she acts as if she wants him to.

Whether it is the boy or the girl who starts behavior that can so easily lead to serious sin, it is irresponsible and unfair, and it surely doesn't show real friendship. True friends don't make it hard for each other to do the right thing.

God's laws are perfect. They protect us, make us wise, and give us joy and light.
Psalm 19:7,8

Whatever you do or say, let it be as a representative of the Lord Jesus, and come with him into the presence of God the Father to give him your thanks.
Colossians 3:17